JOY

A MOTHER'S LOVE KNOWS NO BOUNDARIES

BY DIANE LEYDEN

Boulevard Books

The New Face of Publishing

www.BoulevardBooks.org

ABOUT THE AUTHOR

Diane Leyden was born on June 23, 1947, in Brooklyn, New York. She attended Lincoln High School and then went on to attend Kingsborough Community College. She married Howard Leyden on March 9, 1969. In her early years she worked for the Jewish Welfare Board as an administrative assistant. After giving birth she became a stay at home mom and raised her 2 daughters. In the early 1990s she returned to the workforce as a Chiropractic Assistant. Diane enjoyed trips to Atlantic City and many summers in the Catskill Mountains making memories with family and friends. Devoted to her husband and children, she always put them first. This did not leave much time for her to pursue her own passions and dreams. Diane passed away on February 20,1997. She was only 49 years old. Diane always had a desire to write a book. Sadly it was not until she passed away that her daughters discovered she had actually done so. It has been their goal to fulfill their mother's dream. This book is the precious gift that she left behind. Her legacy continues to live on.

FOREWORD

Our mother, Diane Leyden, was a loving, strong, selfless, kind, and witty woman. She was a devoted wife and mother. Diane Leyden was taken from us too young and too soon. She passed away on February 20th, 1997 at the age of 49. 2017 marks twenty years since her passing. She died from breast cancer yet no one, family nor friend, knew that she was battling this awful disease alone. While we watched our mother wither away, she insisted her weight loss was from stress and depression. Paralyzed by fear she was unwilling to see a doctor. A fear that we had not realized ran so deep. She convinced us and herself that she would be fine.

As weeks went on she became more ill, still insisting she was going to be okay and that we shouldn't worry about her. Despite her efforts, she eventually had to be taken by ambulance to the hospital. Our father called us and we immediately left college to drive home to be with her. As we walked into our house, our father had the daunting task of telling us that our beloved mother and his devoted wife was dying. This is a memory we will never forget. We went quickly to the hospital to find her heavily sedated and in organ failure. We sat vigil at her bedside talking to her and hoping that she heard us. We told her that she didn't have to fight anymore and that we would be okay. We watched as she took her last breath, a memory that is forever etched in our minds. We could only hope that she was now at peace.

She suffered in silence for months with unimaginable pain as the cancer took over her body. The selfless woman that she was, she would always reassure us that she would be okay. She did not want to disrupt our lives. She did not want us coming home from college. She only wanted to spare us the pain of watching her suffer. Countless family members and friends were devastated and found her passing difficult to comprehend. Those who truly knew our mother, Diane Leyden, realized that with her strong will and selfless personality, she truly thought she could fight this battle alone. The enormity of the situation however spiraled out of control and it proved to be too late.

The days that followed were filled with disbelief, sadness, frustration and anger. She was gone and how were we going to get through the rest of that day, that week, the rest of our life without our mother. We stayed home from college for a few weeks but we soon realized that we needed to go back. She was always so proud of us, especially our academic accomplishments that we knew she would have been heartbroken if we didn't finish college. With the strength that we knew she fought with everyday, we both returned to school.

In the months following her untimely death, we gained strength and resilience that we only later realized that she instilled in us. At some point during the weeks to follow, we were going through her belongings and found her electric typewriter. With it we found a manuscript that she had written when she was 34 years old. We vaguely remember her talking about wanting to write a book over the years, but we had not known that she had actually done so.

This treasured, precious gift was written by our mother. It represents how a mother's love knows no boundaries. With each line that you read, you can hear her voice and feel her quick wit and humor seeping through. We have held onto this book for twenty years, always thinking that one day we would be able to fulfill her dream and have it published.

Her book is a lighthearted version of her journey from conception to birth and everything in between. She uses wit and humor to tell her story as it occurred in the 1970's. As our mother, Diane Leyden, always said, "leave them laughing," this is exactly what this book does.

Six days before she died we both received Valentine's Day cards and as always she signed it, "I love you forever and a day." We have held onto this sentiment, knowing that she is always with us. We realize that the way in which she lived her life, with enormous strength and courage, is forever instilled in us and we are forever grateful.

Even after all of these years and being mothers ourselves, we will always feel the void of her absence. When you lose a parent it leaves a permanent hole in your heart. We will always be saddened and frustrated for her that she suffered in silence all alone, but also know and understand why.

Our mother, Diane Leyden, was the epitome of selflessness and a mother's love.

As you (and Daddy- passed away 2014) watch over us, always know that you are greatly missed.

TO OUR MOTHER DIANE LEYDEN, YOU ALWAYS PUT OTHERS FIRST. YOU LOVED US UNCONDITIONALLY AND ALWAYS MADE SURE WE KNEW IT. WE WANT TO THANK YOU FOR ALL THAT YOU DID FOR US AND FOR LEAVING US THIS PRECIOUS GIFT. WE MISS YOU MORE THAN WORDS CAN SAY. WE WILL ALWAYS LOVE YOU FOREVER AND A DAY...

YOUR DAUGHTERS-
TAMMY JOY VINCIGUERRA
HOPE ROBYN FULLER

Chapter 1

Hi. Let me introduce myself. I am a 34 year old suburban housewife, mother of two, wife of one. Something was missing in my life and I have always had a fantasy that one day I would write a book. I have always had the desire to write, but I always came up with an excuse that prevented me from doing so.

My main excuse was that I only had a manual typewriter and could not type well on it. So I made a deal with myself. I said that when I went to Atlantic City, if I won enough money to buy a portable electric typewriter I would attempt to write a book.

I knew the odds of my winning money weren't too good so I felt I had made a safe bet. Wrong! I went to A.C. and couldn't do a thing wrong. I had made enough money to buy the typewriter, even pay for the tax! It must have been fate and my fantasy of writing a book had begun.

As I sit before my new electric typewriter thoughts are whizzing through my mind faster than the speed of light. I want to write badly, so badly that all the thoughts are blending into one idea. I must get a hold of myself to maintain my sanity. First, what should I write about?

I want to write about something that will interest people, but what? Whenever I listen to comics do routines, the best routines are those that related to themselves. I just answered my first question. I will write about something that I personally know about. Now, we come to another problem, I know about a lot of things!

I could write about my relatives or friends, but WHY get involved in slander lawsuits. To play it safe, I would write about something that is near and dear to me- ME.

And the whole idea of this book-STARTED WITH SEX.

Chapter 2

Let's start at the beginning. I was married March 9th, 1969. (This may be a little dull, but I did say I had to start at the beginning.) As most young couples feel at the beginning of marriage, they don't want to start a family right away. Being average, it wasn't until about 3 ½ years later that I became pregnant.

My daughter's life started at a hotel in upstate New York on the 4th of July. The reason I am sure of this is because the rest of that summer we shared a bungalow with my parents and the walls were so thin that if somebody sneezed next door WE would say "God Bless You." Of course my husband and I didn't have the nerve to fool around. So, we started the summer of 1972 off with a bang on the Fourth of July at the hotel.

I had taken the summer off to try and relax. Sure enough about three weeks after the fourth, it hit me like a bomb. It's called morning sickness, except my sickness had no time limit and lasted all night and all day. I would get up in the morning and wish it was night, although I couldn't figure out why because I felt just as sick at night as I did during the day.

When you are feeling this way it was not such a terrific idea to be around your mother who was always offering you food. I did not want to tell my parents and get their hopes up that I may be pregnant, so would I just lay around like a dead one for three weeks. Of course, I am the type of person who doesn't have any confidence in themselves, so I really did think, "How could I be pregnant?" I was convinced this awful sick feeling must be CANCER. In three weeks, I had lost over 10 pounds, now my weight was just over 100. Boy, was I sick. I could not stand to be in a room where there was food or to be with people who talked about food. I felt that I constantly had sawdust in my mouth. All I wanted to do was sleep, and that was pretty hard when my mother was constantly following me around with something to eat.

This horrible episode lasted until I finally consented to come home for a few days and see a doctor. Being the brave soul that I am, I had NEVER been to a gynecologist before. By the time my husband and I arrived at the office

I was so weak from nerves and not eating that I was barely able to stand up myself.

The nurse said the information she had to take would only take a few minutes, but in the condition I was in a few minutes seemed like forever. At the end of the questioning, she gave me a pathetic look and said, "Tsk, tsk." This was sure to be the final sign that pregnancy WAS NOT the cause of my strange illness, but that CANCER was.

I was ushered into a room and was told very politely to STRIP, just like a drill sergeant in the Marines would give the order to KILL. I sheepishly said, "EVERYTHING?" The nurse replied, "You can leave your earrings." It was just adding insult to injury because I wasn't wearing any earrings! Now, enters the doctor. Just like Loretta Young he swept into the office, his white coat flapping in the breeze. With him was a nurse, young enough to be in the sixth grade (it seemed to ME). Now he says, while looking at my chart, "What have we here?" I thought it would be easy for him to see that before him was a girl at least 10 pounds underweight looking like she had just died, but at this point I was so nervous I broke out in a rash over my entire body. Now, I figured I have made this doctor famous. "Gynecologist finds cancer victim with leprosy," the headlines of the medical journal would read.

He now washes his hands, puts on the rubber glove, (I thought maybe, he wanted to wash some dishes, wishful thinking.) He then says those famous words all of us women love to hear, RELAX. Sure buddy, I wanted to say, you relax with what looks like a fist of five fingers just about to enter my private area.

Now, this preteen nurse bends over and whispers in my ear, as she is firmly holding my hand, "Is this your first time at the gynecologist?" "Of course not," so I lied. At this point I don't know who was in more pain, this future Florence Nightingale or me. You see, I was squeezing her hand so tightly that I must have stopped the blood from circulating. She was yelling, "Please stop." I thought, "Gee she is on my side asking the doctor to stop." Little did I know she was addressing herself to me. When he finished probing that was when I let go of this ex-nurses hand. I heard that was her first and last internal.

When Doctor Frankenstein (only kidding) was finished, I thought he would say I was very sick, but instead he said as all doctors do, I will see you in my office after you get dressed. Well, of course, he wanted me to get dressed he had already seen more than anyone else had.

After about what seemed to be three days (only about 15 minutes) he called me and my husband into his office. I figured he was about to say, only six months to live. He said, "What your wife has isn't that rare, however it is highly contagious and can only be caught through sex. It is called PREGNANCY." After a quick whiff of smelling salts, I was able to concentrate on what he was saying. He told me to eat well, at which point I gagged and reached for the trusty saltine crackers which I could not be more than 10 feet from at all times. Saltine crackers are to a pregnant woman like Nitro tablets are to a heart patient. He then said, "Good luck, I will see you in one month."

Chapter 3

Now the next step was to go back Upstate New York and proceed to tell my parents the fate of my so-called illness. Believe it or not I was embarrassed to admit to my parents that we actually FOOLED AROUND and the result was pregnancy.

My mother took it quite well as I had expected. My father's eyes were filled with tears and he was of course concerned that we could not afford such a luxury as a baby. After much discussion we finally got him to realize that we weren't exactly living on skid row.

The rest of the summer went pretty well, or should I say pretty "sick". Everyone said that soon I would be feeling better. What is soon for some is an eternity for others. After Labor Day I went back to work. I wanted to keep the pregnancy a secret for awhile, but my while was about 30 seconds. As soon as I walked into the office I blurted it out. As my third month began my cravings started. I ate nothing all day, but by three o'clock I had to have a chocolate malted and a piece of chocolate layer cake. I ate so much chocolate I thought the baby would turn out to be brown. Most of the women I worked with were on Weight Watchers, so they weren't too thrilled with the fact that my afternoon snack consisted of more calories than they were allowed for the entire week.

Work kept my mind occupied so that I did not realize how nauseous I was most of the time. At the end of each week when it came to cleaning out my typewriter I realized that all the crumbs from the saltine crackers found their way to the bottom of the typewriter's carriage. The first time this was brought to my attention is when I needed the IBM man to come because only half of the letters I was typing were coming out. After cleaning out my typewriter he said, "So what month are you in?" I looked at him with quite a puzzling look and then he showed me a cup full of cracker crumbs.

After work I was so exhausted that I felt the rush hour crowd just push me along to the nearest subway. Half the time I didn't even care if it were the right one. At the beginning, of course, you don't look pregnant, just sickly. Rush hour crowds ignored me until my friend and I devised a fool proof system of getting seats. We would get pushed on the subway and stand over people seated holding onto the straps above. Then in a loud voice my friend said, "So, what did the doctor say?" Looking the way I did my answer was very conceivable. I would say, "He doesn't say much except I should try and stay out of large crowds because there are many people who do not have a natural immunity to my disease. But, because of the large medical bills, I am forced to continue to work." This short but convincing conversation worked 9 out of 10 times. The people in front of us would very hurriedly leave the car we were in. The only problem we had was we had to make sure we didn't pull this snow job on the same people. We had become well known on the BMT Brighton Line. In fact, several times when we entered the car we would automatically get seats. As I began to look like I was with child, people were a little more compassionate and gave me their seat.

Each time I got off the train in my third month I would buy 1 beef tomato. I would go home and eat it with a hard boiled egg and about 30 seconds later would meet my friend the toilet bowl and give it right back. My husband worked late so for the next few months the only time we got to talk was if he called me at work. I went to sleep at 7pm and got up the next morning to go to work.

Chapter 4

Mentally I was much more prepared for my second visit to the doctor, basically because I knew that I could keep my clothes on. On a Saturday morning at the beginning of my fourth month I went downstairs about 1 hour before my appointment to wait for the bus. It would take me directly to the doctor's office. That is if it ever showed up. I waited about 45 minutes and not a bus in sight. During the time I was waiting for the bus a man about my age was standing with me. I kept on commenting how long it was taking for the bus to come. He informed me that this line was famous for not running on time. He was quite pleasant. Now it was about 10:55 and I had an 11:OO appointment. I was quickly losing my cool. With that, a car pulls up to pick up my bus partner. Out of the clear blue skies I heard a voice saying, "I have to go to a doctor's appointment, would you be going my way?" I looked around and to my astonishment it was me who was talking. The driver said, "Sure get in." I think when you become pregnant besides your body changing there is a change in your mind, YOU LOSE IT. I would never under normal circumstances have asked for a ride. A special power came over me as if to say YOU CAN DO ANYTHING NOW AND GET AWAY WITH IT.

I was quite relaxed in the car for about one minute until the conversation between these two men changed from how's the family to their deep discussion about their guns. My whole life passed before my eyes. I would never know what I could have given birth to. To make matters worse I had forgotten my trusty saltine crackers. A normal 10 minute ride turned into 35 minutes because we got stopped at every light. At the end of the ride, the driver turned to me and said, "You look a little nervous. Did our conversation bother you?" As I had my hand on the door and was about to make a quick getaway, I said, "Yes." He then said, "You shouldn't ask strangers for rides. We are police officers and we wouldn't recommend that you do this too often." I swore that I had NEVER done it before and would not take any chances in the future.

Chapter 5

As I approached the doctor's office I saw a group of extremely pregnant women standing before me. This was my first morning appointment and I was informed that it was on a first come first serve basis. When the nurse came and finally opened the door all these fat bellies started to push towards me. I felt like a football player when he has the ball and everyone else wants it. I quickly got out of their way, so of course my name ended up on the bottom of the list.

It was an experience just sitting there. When I walked in I knew nothing about having a baby and when I walked out I knew so much I was a nervous wreck. After a woman gave birth she is so well advised (or so she thinks) that you begin to wonder why you are giving the doctor $750 when any of these girls knew so much they could do the delivery. I heard of labor lasting anywhere from ½ hour at which point the woman gave birth in the elevator to five days of such awful pain that you actually wish you were dead. As I am sitting there, one of the women said very calmly that her water just broke. Later I found out this was her sixth child. The nurses were frantic, not because this woman was uncomfortable, but because the chairs had just been reupholstered and the carpeting was new. Instead of coming out to bring the woman into the examining room they ran for paper towel and a mop. The woman was finally ushered into the inner office never to be heard from again.

My name was finally called. The nurse weighed me and then asked me for my urine bottle. Due to the wonderful car ride I had and all the scrounging in my purse to try and find crackers, I was only able to recover about two drops of urine in the bottle and the rest was at the bottom of my bag. My weight was good and the little urine that was saved thankfully was fine too.

The doctor made his entrance. He tested my blood pressure and because of the way the day had already gone I thought I would break the machine. To my surprise, it was perfect. He said all is good, keep it up and I will see you in one month.

To play it safe I took a cab ride home. Safe I thought. The cab driver was a maniac. After I got out of the cab, I questioned whether or not someone had a contract put out on my life. He went through lights, around cars and at one point I closed my eyes and thought we were going to wind up under a tractor trailer truck. I was truly relieved to get home. I nibbled my crackers and went to sleep.

Chapter 6

At the beginning of my fourth month I began to feel flip flops moving inside of me. It was the nicest feeling in the world to know that I had something to do (a lot to do) with someone growing inside of me.

My morning, afternoon, and night sickness began leaving me during my fifth month. It was great to wake up and know that the first thing I didn't have to do was fling myself over the toilet bowl. I started going to work like a trooper. Previously, I would arrive at work 45 minutes late and sign in with a huge TD next to my name. TD stood for transportation delay. It was getting increasingly more difficult to explain to the bosses why I was always late and the other employees who took the same train arrived on time. I have to admit they had been pretty patient with me. Each morning I would be greeted by the office manager who would say, "Don't you think that now that you are pregnant you should be staying home taking care of yourself?" I always replied, "You take such good care of me here. You are constantly passing my desk and making sure that I am alright. I rather be here than home alone." I knew darn well that she was always walking by my desk checking on me to make sure that I was there and working!

The management was quite relieved to learn that I would be leaving at the end of my 7th month. It was customary for someone who was leaving to make a small party. Being that the office staff chipped in and bought me so many things for the baby, the least I could do was make a small party. By the time I arrived at the office that is all it turned out to be.

That morning my husband drove me and my friend to the express bus stop where we got the bus that was to take us directly to our office. Traffic was very heavy that day and we got stuck in the tunnel for 45 minutes. I was so happy that on my last day at work when I signed TD next to my name, it was really true. My husband had bought about two pounds of assorted cookies. The fact that we were on the bus so long made us hungry. Little by little, then a lot by a lot, we ate the cookies. We were so busy eating the cookies that we missed our stop. We couldn't get a cab and had to walk several blocks back to our office.

When it came time to put out the cookies, all that was left was the chocolate stained wax paper the cookies were wrapped in. You see, when we were eating the cookies we didn't open the box, we just slid the cookies out. So, it was a surprise when the box was opened that not much was left. Thankfully, there was plenty of liquor. We set out the liquor at 11:00am and by 11:30am news spread fast and 99% of my fellow coworkers were drinking their hearts out. With no cookies to absorb the liquor, within no time the place was one big New Year's Eve celebration without Guy Lombardo.

No one went out to lunch that day. In fact, no one even worked that day. Luckily, most of the employees were union workers. After about three hours we realized that no calls had come in all day. We soon realized the reason for that was the switch board operator was under one of the desks with an empty bottle of gin. My little party unofficially closed down the office for the day. After many teary good-byes, I left to start my new life at home as mother to be. I took the subway home and made a grand exit. I announced that they had just discovered a miracle that would cure my illness, it was "a sense of humor" and I exited laughing.

Chapter 7

The night before the end of my 7th month doctor's appointment my husband brought home a dozen Dunkin Donuts for company I was expecting for lunch. I couldn't sleep well that night. So it wasn't a total loss, being that I was awake, I ate all the doughnuts. I knew that it was me eating, but it was something I couldn't stop nor had the desire to do so.

I awoke in the morning, showered, got dressed and proceeded to wobble to the bus stop. It was funny, the previous day I didn't wobble. It must have been the doughnuts as well as the cookies that I had consumed during the previous week. My doctor was very strict when it came to gaining weight. He would scream and embarrass you so that you would immediately swear on anything that was holy that no junk food would ever enter your mouth again. I knew I had gained quite a bit and I knew that I was in for a bad visit with the doctor.

When I arrived at the office, as expected was the line of fat stomachs. The nurse came out and said the doctor would be a little late in starting to call us in. It was quiet in the office except for the usual, have I got a story for you talk. Then out of the clear blue skies, we heard a baby crying. At least 10 girls at one time turned white as a ghost and lunged toward the bathroom. The bathroom was hardly large enough for one of us, so 10 at one time was like a large can of sardines being shoved into a smaller can. None of us were able to talk. First, a woman's water broke a few months ago and now a baby being born. Then, ten minutes later, a woman comes walking out, her husband behind her holding a baby. Boy, that was a fast recovery. I thought to myself, "Giving birth was really easy." (HA!) The doctor stepped out into the outer office where we were all seated, looked at our faces and realized an explanation was in order. He had just preformed a circumcision on the baby. It was NOT a delivery.

This incident made me forget for the time being of my weight problem. Not for long though. The nurse called my name and when I stepped on the scale she took a double take. She had me step off and readjusted the scale and tried weighing me again. She looked at me with pathetic eyes and said, "Good Luck."

The doctor walked in smiling. I tried smiling back, but because I knew what was in store for me the only reaction I had was for tears to come flowing out of my eyes. He looked at my chart and said, "Now I see the cause for the tears." He went on and on about the obesity that had come upon me. He then said, "I will see you in my office."

I went in and he hit me with something else to worry about. He said that I had the RH factor, an issue with my blood and that my blood would need to be tested several times during the next couple of weeks. Then I asked the question that I soon found that you should never ask a doctor. I asked, "What is the worst thing that could happen to the baby if our blood does not match?" He said, "The baby could be still born." At that point my blood pressure must have gone sky high because it wasn't until I felt the nurse rubbing the back of my neck did I hear what else the doctor with such compassion had to say. "It is unlikely it will happen and there is nothing to worry about." Another thrilling visit to the doctor and I was relieved to be heading home.

Chapter 8

My days were always the same. I became first a game show freak and then after lunch addicted to those incredible soap operas. I tried spending time with my friends that had children, but I got too nervous being around children. I was having trouble imagining myself as a mother.

Every time I went to put something illegal into my mouth, I remembered Dr. Beast. I was now limited to only food shopping because everything I saw I wanted to eat. My husband ate a lot during those last two months.

Due to the fact that I was limited by the doctor to what I could eat, my patience became limited too. When you are pregnant your adrenalin seems to flow faster than usual and give you extra strength. One night I had an argument with my husband over something ridiculous. Now it was ridiculous, but then it was traumatic. I was so angry I picked up a fork and bent it. Apparently my husband thought it was funny and began to laugh. Here is a warning to all men, don't ever laugh at a pregnant woman. He infuriated me. I took the fork and threw it. I knew I couldn't hit him from where he was standing, but I did not count on the fact that he would start walking towards me. The fork landed in the calf of his leg. The blood started to trickle down. I became hysterical, crying and thinking, not that he could really be hurt, but how will I explain this to our parents. Well, thankfully I did not have to explain anything because he was not badly hurt. In fact, if our parents read this now it will be the first time they have heard about it.

Chapter 9

I found out that when you are pregnant you can get away with things that normally would not work. A good example of that is when my husband and myself went to buy a new car. I was now very huge (thanks to all the doughnuts I have eaten along the way.) When we entered the car dealership the salesmen ascended upon us as though we were the queen bee and they were the bees.

We finally settled on this poor schnook sitting at his desk having an argument with his girlfriend on the phone. We asked him if he could help us and he jumped as high as a stalk of corn at its peak. He showed us many models and insisted that we sit in every car. This took awhile because of me, DUMBO. I slid in and out of so many cars that day that the seat of my pants was shiny enough to see yourself. If you wanted to stoop that low!

About two hours later, we found ourselves sitting at the salesman's desk. He was so unorganized it was pathetic. We decided on the floor model. The only problem was it came with extras we did not necessarily want. He desperately wanted to make the sale so after awhile we had him eating out of the palm of our hands.

Every time he mentioned another extra, I would grab my protruding stomach and moan. He would say, "O.K no charge." I made him so nervous that half the time he didn't know what he was saying. After about one hour of moaning and groaning the deal was final, except for the fact that his manager had to sign the final agreement. As he was leaving to get the paperwork signed, I said, "You better hurry it could be any time now." He was back in no time.

This was on a Friday. The car had to be picked up on Monday. We had to rush to the bank and withdraw the money. We were so excited about the car and the baby that we did not realize that we could have paid by check instead of making a huge withdrawal of cash. So, there we were leaving the bank with some $3000+ in our possession. By the time we got home we were paranoid. We felt that everyone and their brother were following us.

We had to go through an entire weekend with this money. We had the perfect place to hide it. We wrapped thirty, one hundred dollar bills in tin foil and put them in the freezer. I am happy to report that the freezer turned out to be a safe place. Monday morning we got up bright and early to pick up our new car. Our old car was already sold so we had to find a way to get to the car dealership. I refused to take a cab. I hadn't been in one since that time I took it home from the doctor's office several months prior. I insisted on taking two buses. My husband, afraid of my temper, consented to go along with my wishes. He went to the freezer, grabbed the package of money and off we went. It was a good thing he took the tin foil off in the elevator, because in his haste he grabbed a package of lamb chops instead of the money.

We made it to the car dealership and we were greeted with a not so happy salesman. He informed us that all the extras that he had given us were now not possible. We told him that we had signed an agreement, left the deposit and they had to give us the car they promised. Now, comes out this giant of a man, the MANAGER. He looked at us and we looked at him. Have you heard of love at first sight, well this was the opposite. His attitude was awful. He said there was no way he would give us the car. We were completely in the right because we had signed the agreement, which he had also signed.

I did not feel like wasting time standing around and arguing, so I started to moan and said, "OH, I think it's TIME." You never saw attitudes change so fast. By no means did they want me to give birth there. They got the keys to the car and off we went, NOT to the hospital, but of course to get something to eat.

Chapter 10

The ninth month started with my weekly visits to the
hospital and blood tests to determine whether or not the
baby was okay due to the issue with my blood.   The
results of the tests always came back good and we were all
relieved. The first visit to the doctor in my ninth month
brought back old memories and trauma of my very first
encounter with Dr. Feelings. After waiting on line as usual
my name was finally called. The nurse checked my urine
specimen and by now I had become a real expert keeping
it in the bottle. My weight was more or less average now
(mostly more, but who cared it was near the end now, one
way or the other). As the nurse was leaving she said that
famous word that immediately made a rash appear over
my entire body, STRIP. This time it was only from the
waist down. What a break I sadly thought.

I carefully climbed up on the table and waited for HIM
to come in. He could have kept me waiting until I went
into labor, but he didn't. He entered with his usual happy
face. He said, "What could you be so allergic to that you
break out into a rash like that?" I replied, "I am allergic to

you and your hand in my private place." He showed absolutely no sign of a sense of humor. He said, "Lay back and relax." You already know how I feel about that, so I will skip the words that went through my mind. He felt the outside of my stomach with one hand while you know where the other hand was. I must admit it was fast. He said, "Get dressed, I will see you in my office." He left me in a fully reclined position on a table that was about two feet wide. In the condition I was in I was not as agile as I used to be. I was completely unable to lift myself up from the table. I tried turning on my side, but then I realized how high off the ground I was and I was afraid of falling. Sure, I thought The Eye Witness News Team would have a wonderful time telling how a pregnant woman died falling off the examining table. I was completely helpless. I figured if I stayed there long enough someone would realize I was missing. Sure enough about ten minutes later, only because they needed the room, a nurse came in and pried me off the table. She escorted me to the doctor's office. I was just about to tell him what I thought about his bedside manner, when I remembered he was the one that would have the last word and he was in control. For once in my life that brave little person inside of me kept her mouth shut.

I did not go home after I left the office. I decided to go out to lunch. I didn't think that was such a big deal. Well, to my parents, husband, friends, and the immediate world, it was a mortal sin. I did not report in to anyone. About three hours later when I arrived at home the phone was practically ringing off the hook. It started with my husband's call. After expressing how he felt about my unexpected lunch, I told him I had nothing to report regarding my doctor's visit. It would have been easier to make a recording of those words because for the next four hours that is all I was saying.

Chapter 11

By now I was really getting good at wobbling and getting on and off a chair or a bed. It should be an Olympic competition for pregnant women. It took so much skill. You would be able to win a blue or a pink ribbon depending on the sex of the child you were having.

As the month went on, the pressure of having something grow in me became very intense. At times the baby would press on a nerve and I was unable to walk. Not that it mattered anyway. I wasn't allowed to go far because I had to be near the phone for my hourly calls from my husband and parents.

The next two visits to the doctor were routine. It was now getting close to my due date and every little pain was timed. I was worried if my water broke in bed I would ruin the mattress, so I took a huge bath towel to bed each night.

My last visit to the doctor was March 26th. He was pleased with my weight which was a miracle in itself. I didn't think anything pleased him except going to the bank and depositing the money all his patients paid him. After the examination, which I was now getting used to, I asked, "Do you know what it is?" He said, "Yes," after a long pause, "A baby." He asked, "When were you due?" I responded, "Two days ago." He replied, "You are going to be late." I thought to myself, I will not dare to express my feelings now, but I did want to know if he had a job moonlighting as a comedian and a fortune teller. After a brief encounter in his office, he said, "See you next week." Not if I can help it, I thought.

At this point of my pregnancy my husband felt it was of the utmost importance for him to follow me wherever I went. If it were possible I think that my husband would have carried me around until I gave birth. I think that ever since the episode with the fork, he treated me with kid gloves for he was in constant fear for his life.

When I walked out into the waiting room filled with about 15 women, from across the room my husband yelled out, "What did he say?" Now you have to picture the way a pregnant woman looks when she is a few days over her due date, HUGE. With a big smile I said, "This doctor must have graduated at the top of his class. He said that I was going to have a baby!" My motto is always leave them laughing and that is what I did when I exited the office.

Chapter 12

On Wednesday, March 28, one of my friends asked me to do her a favor. She had a seven month old baby and she had to go and buy a baby carriage. She asked me if I would walk with her because she needed someone to push the new carriage back. It was quite a walk, but I felt what harm could it do. She bought the carriage and then we began our return journey. I felt we had walked so much we could have been in the Land of Oz and I was looking for the yellow brick road. On the way back we met several of our friends and they walked along with their baby's. I was the only one with a built in carriage. We passed a group of elderly women who passed the time of day by stopping young women with children and admiring them. I was at the end of a line of 8 carriages. There I was, my stomach so big it would reach a destination 3 minutes before I would. When these elderly admirers finally saw me pushing an empty carriage they looked at me bewildered. I said, "The doctor said I should always be prepared it could be any time."

By the time I arrived home, I had worked up such an appetite. I took out a frozen Sara Lee cake and started to nibble. The nibbles soon became large chunks. What had I done! I felt that I had committed a crime. If I would make it to my next doctor's appointment Dr. Weight would kill me. I prayed and I said, "If there is a labor God, please let me go into labor tonight."

Chapter 13

The rest of the evening crept along and before I knew it I heard my husband's key in the door. I had completely forgotten to make him anything for supper. I felt spaced out from all the chocolate cake I had eaten. I must admit, that at that time I had a stomachache. Of course, I thought I felt sick from the cake. The fear of having to be weighed by my doctor made me completely forget that my stomach pains could be labor.

My husband found me on the sofa in the living room unable to lift myself up (a common position I had been caught in more than once). I decided to play the pathetic pregnant woman act. "I am sorry that I did not have anything for you to eat, but I have this sort of pain," I said. Panic immediately set in. He ran to the phone and before I knew it my friend from the floor below was standing there holding her shoes in her hand. I couldn't imagine what she was doing here. She said that we needed a rehearsal. For what, I thought. This isn't an episode of I Love Lucy. I felt that these two were really nervous and I did not want to be part of their rehearsal. I wobbled into the kitchen and started preparing a salad.

The walls were thin in the apartment and I heard every word that they were saying. They both felt that it was TIME. What did they know? With that I felt a different kind of pain. I figured let me give them some good experience in the art of rehearsal. I gave out a little grunt and like two dogs in heat they ran panting into the kitchen. I told them that I had felt a pain. They both went scrambling for the stopwatch. I said, "Listen, I don't plan on running in a race, what's with the watch?" "To time your pain so tell me when it's over," my friend answered. "About two minutes ago," I replied.

I gave my husband a salad and asked him to eat it in the other room. My friend, god bless her, followed me around wherever I went, waiting for the next pain. I put my foot down though, when she wanted to follow me into the bathroom. I decided now, to keep my pains to myself. They came and went for awhile, but then, they started to get very strong, and I could no longer keep it a secret. I told my friend not to tell my husband. By now she thought she was a midwife and had everything under control. The contractions were coming about every five minutes. I then discovered why they call them "contractions". It is because your whole entire body feels like it is folding up or contracting.

At this point we felt it was time to call the doctor. I bravely dialed his office number and got in touch with the doctor's service. They asked me my name, address, phone number and what the problem was. I said, "I think I am in labor, the pains are coming every five minutes." "Why didn't you say that in the first place," a woman screeched back at me. As politely as I could I replied, "Because you did not ask." Then she hit me with what felt like a bomb. She told me that my doctor was out of town and the associate was on call. She gave me his number and I hung up deeply in shock. How could I possibly call this strange person? I begged my friend the midwife to call for me, but all of a sudden she lost interest in me. I was a big girl now, about to become a mother, and I had to start taking responsibilities of motherhood into my own hands.

It was now about 12:30am. I not only had to call a strange doctor but I had to wake him up to boot. I nervously dialed the numbers and as the phone rang I thought what happens if his wife answers, just ask for the doctor I quickly figured out. One thing went my way, he answered. I started to explain, in detail why I was calling. I neglected to give him my name and by the time he was able to get a word in I was practically too much out of breath to answer him. I barely got out Diane, when he said "Leyden". I felt like I just won the top prize on a game show. "He knows my name," I yelled. Both my husband and friend looked at me if I needed a psychiatrist rather than a gynecologist. He calmed me down and told me he had my chart in front of him because my regular doctor felt that I would be delivering soon. He asked, "How far apart are the pains?" I replied, "About five minutes." He asked, "How long do the contractions last?" That's where my calmness ended. I shyly said, "I don't know." Time the next contraction and give me a call back," he replied.

The next contraction came practically simultaneously to hanging up the phone. It lasted 30 seconds. I was too embarrassed to call right back so I waited for two more contractions. By now they lasted for 45 seconds. My audience insisted now was the time to make the call. The first few minutes of my conversation with the doctor I was apologizing for bothering him and disturbing his sleep. When I told him the contractions were lasting 45 seconds, he said, "Get right over to the hospital." The words reverberated in my head for a few minutes before I realized he was serious.

All the nightgowns I had carefully hanging up so they wouldn't get creased my friend stuffed into my suitcase. It did turn out to be like an episode of I LOVE LUCY, because believe it or not, they ran out, slammed the door and left me in the bathroom. When I realized I was alone I left the apartment and went outside in front of the building. I found these two "Towers of Strength" looking up and down the street for our car. They were convinced our car had been stolen because there wasn't a blue Catalina Pontiac in sight. "Of course not," I screamed. Two days ago we withdrew all that money from the bank. We proceeded to the car dealer and bought a brand new beige Ford Maverick, and there it is. Both of them were too nervous to be embarrassed. They grabbed me by my arms and literally threw me into the car.

Chapter 14

We made several practice runs to the hospital, but of course they were to no avail because the father-to-be lost all sense of directions. His greatest expectation was to be able to honk his horn, go through all the lights, be stopped by a police car and get a police escort to the hospital. Poor, honey, nothing like that at all happened. There were no cars out on the road at all. All the lights were green and even though he was going faster than he should have been, there were no police cars out either. After a few wrong turns, we finally arrived at the hospital.

We walked into the hospital. I should say, I walked, and the other two ran. They reached the admitting desk and were asked, "What can I do for you?" They both shouted we're expecting. When they turned around to look at me, I wasn't there. I had gotten an attack of a nervous stomach and I just about made it to the bathroom. I told them I was sorry for not warning them of my short disappearance, but I had no choice. They took the information needed and then a huge nurse dressed in a green operating cap and gown came out to get me. I handed my wedding ring over to my husband, kissed my friend and then my husband good-bye and started on an adventure which now I can laugh about, but then only tears were appropriate.

Chapter 15

They led me into a room with a bed, a sink and some strange looking machinery. The nurse handed me a gown and said, of course, STRIP. The doctor was expected in momentarily. I was laying there for such a long time. I had time to remember everything that ever happened to me from age two and up. I was expecting my doctor when this pudgy little boy all dressed in white walks in. He looked like the Pillsbury Dough Boy.

He introduced himself. I thought nice to meet you, but get the hell out of here and send in my doctor. He said he would give me an internal to determine whether or not I was ready. I said, "Take my word for it, I'm ready." He said, "I am a professional and I am the one to decide." I said to him, "I am the mother-to-be and I am feeling all the pain and the pressure and the pulling inside of me." He then started to answer me back and I knew at that point I wasn't going to get anywhere with him, so I said, "Do what you have to."

I got the first hint that I was in trouble when he went to put the plastic glove on and he shoved his hand right through it. He had a big smirk on his face as he reached for another glove. He came towards me, raised my legs and started doing what he said he had to. I will leave out the gory details, use your imagination. This little creep didn't even have the decency to say "Relax". He shoved his hand so far up that I saw stars. My first reflex was to grab his hand, and that is what I did, except I did it with my nails. He yelled, and said, "Get your hands off of me." I replied, "As soon as you get your hand out of me." He did and I did. He had blood dripping down his hand, not from the internal he gave me, but from the external I gave him on his hand and with my nails. He did not even wait to tell me what was going on, he exited from the room as if his shoes were on fire.

I lay there and all there was to do was feel my contractions and listen to the moaning, groaning and screaming coming from the surrounding labor rooms. It is funny, but when a woman is in labor she has the strong urge to curse her husband, and call for her mother, and boy, did I hear cursing. I thought to myself that no matter how bad it gets, I would not stoop to that level. (Ha!)

Laying there, minding my own business all of a sudden I felt this strange sensation from between my legs. I felt that this could be what happens when your water breaks. I called for the nurse, first in a whisper, then in a normal voice and then after about 10 minutes, in a loud scream. Finally, in came a nurse. I said, "I think my water broke." She picked up the cover, looked and then walked out. I thought to myself that this place must be run by deaf mutes. When you call them they don't hear you and then when you finally get their attention and ask them a question, they look at you and walk away. I was flabbergasted. There I was all alone wearing a stiff paper like hospital gown. As if that wasn't bad enough, now I was laying in a substance which had been inside of me for nine months. I called again, and a very sweet nurse came in and put some towels under me. I thought to myself, she'll never keep this job she's too nice.

After about one half hour, the doughboy stopped by, his hand all bandaged, he said he was leaving for the night. No great loss, I thought. I had to go to the bathroom. I managed to get off the bed, and with a kind of a wobbly hop got across the room. As I reached the bathroom, the door to the adjourning room was opened. I made the mistake of looking in. There was a doctor in there with another woman and I did not like what I saw. He was probing with one had while a nurse was giving this poor soul a shot and the woman was screaming on the top of her lungs. I forgot all about the fact that I had to go to the bathroom and raced as fast as I could back to my slab they called a bed.

I thought that I would get a moments peace, but I was wrong. In came a nurse with a tray containing a razor, a pan of water and a bar of soap. She informed me that she was there to shave me. I figured, how bad could that be once you got passed the embarrassing part. Things went along pretty well until she got too close to my hemorrhoids, a condition that I got during pregnancy. I yelled and she said, "Oh I see you have hemorrhoids." I answered, "One less now, thanks to you." She wished me luck and left. At that point, I accepted her luck because I knew that I could use all the luck I could get.

All this time I was there, I was asking when my doctor would be in to see me. They told me there was plenty of time. Every time I told them I had a contraction, they examined me and said I didn't. I thought to myself, who should know better, them or me. I heard some muffled voices out in the hall about some poor girl who had to be watched because she had a rare type blood and may need a transfusion because the baby wasn't dropping and there could be fetal distress. I thought to myself, "Poor girl." I did I know that they were talking about me!

Chapter 16

By this time, it is only 3:30 a.m. I have only been in the hospital for about two hours. This had definitely been the longest two hours in history. I was sure I would read about this record in the Guinness Book.

The contractions were still coming about every five minutes, but lasting longer. I had caught the attention of a nurse passing by only by coughing so loudly that I thought I had relocated my tonsils. She came in, I asked her if it were possible for her to have my husband come in for a few minutes. She said that she would find out. Minutes later she came in to tell me that they had sent my husband home because I would not deliver for about 24 more hours. I couldn't understand why they sent him home, not me. The fact that now I was all alone in the hospital made me cry. How would I possibly be able to withstand another 24 hours of this torture? Now I began to realize how easy it was to call for your mother for help and start cursing your husband.

A group of doctors marched into the room and began poking me here and there. It wasn't the here that bothered me but I did not like the there. I was now up to my sixth internal in the last two hours. They started to attach the strange machinery that I had noticed in the room to my stomach. Within seconds, I heard a thump, thump, thump sound. They said this was the sound of my baby's heart. I told them that instead of the thump sound couldn't they do something so that the baby would come out and I could hear the crying sound instead. They all just looked at me. Out in the hall I heard muffled voices again, but this time could not understand what they were saying. Within seconds, though, I found out the outcome of their examination. They said that I had to be taken for x-rays.

I was stunned. They explained that they baby was stuck under a rib and would not come down. If the x-rays showed that there could be no way for the baby to come down by itself, then I would need a C-Section.

Oh my God, what else could they hit me with. My greatest fear about having a baby was that I would need a C-Section and from the spinal they would have to give me I would have a migraine headache for the rest of my life. The headache was already starting.

A large male nurse came in all dressed in white. This one looked like a Good Humor Man. He was wheeling a stretcher. He put it beside me and told me to hop on. By the look on my face, he knew I was a hopeless case. He called for some help and about three or four people rolled me on this ice cold table. He was really quite pleasant and wanted to know all about me. I told him that there was nothing to know and please shut up. From then on, the trip got a little bumpy. I think every opportunity he had to make a sharp turn he did. At the end of the line, I asked him for his name and license plate number.

There were other people ahead of me and then all of a sudden a nurse frantically said to take me first because it is an emergency. To put it mildly they scared the pants off of me, because they abruptly started to push my stretcher into the x-ray room. Oh God, I thought out loud, I'm the emergency.

They wheeled me into an all white room with a gigantic x-ray machine. The technician walked over to me and again asked the impossible for me to get on the table. I told him if you have about two hours, I will do it myself, but if there is any kind of hurry, you'd better get someone to help me. That is just what he did. These three tough looking aids came towards me. They looked like a goon squad. They flipped me over like a pancake and I found myself on the x-ray table. Remember, about two hours before my water broke, well it doesn't plug itself up once it gets started, it keeps rolling along, like Old Man River. There I was completely humiliated, practically naked and this substance running out between my legs. At that point, the technician turns to me and tells me how I am making a mess on the floor. I said to him, "If you would give me a pail and a mop I'd be glad to clean it up." He ignored my so-called sense of humor and proceeded to go ahead with what he gets paid for.

He turned me over on my side, took a huge stick, propped my legs upward and put the stick in between my legs to keep them apart. He said, "Don't move or I'll have to do it again." It is practically impossible for anyone to tell a pregnant woman in labor not to move, because when the contractions come, you can't help but move. Well, this happened about five times. He was getting annoyed with me as if it were my fault. Again, he said,

"What a mess." I chose to ignore him this time. Every time he had to replace the stick, he jabbed me a little harder. Finally, it was over. I was placed back on the stretcher and moved into the hall. After about 15 minutes, he came out with the results. He whispered, "What do you want, a boy or a girl?" I told him it didn't matter. "Do you know I asked?" He shook his head affirmatively. "What is it?" I asked. "A baby," he replied.

By this time, I was completely fed up with Mr. Clean. I said, "I have to throw up." He said, "You can't, you'll mess everything up." I then started to gag. He ran for a small bowl. He placed it by my mouth and I started to spit just like a baby who has had enough to eat and spits out his food. "That's no way to throw up," he said. "I don't tell you how to take x-rays, so don't tell me how to throw up," I replied. I was then quickly whisked away from him and brought back to my labor room.

Chapter 17

I was greeted in the labor room by a group of grim looking doctors and nurses, none of whom were familiar to me. I demanded to know where my doctor was and they told me that they had called him and finally he was on his way.

One of the doctors came towards me and told me that I would need a C-section. "No way," I said. There seemed to have been a communication problem because they proceeded to go ahead with the things that had to be done. They reattached the fetal monitor to me. A nice heartbeat I was told. It definitely has the heartbeat of a boy. From then on, all these geniuses of the medical profession told me it was a boy.

Then in walked the same nurse who had groomed me earlier, remember the one who removed the hemorrhoid free of charge. She informed me that now she had to shave my stomach. I insisted that there was no need for that because there was no way they were going to cut me. I thought I made myself clearly understood, but I was wrong. She removed my gown and on she went with the razor. She reminded me of Jack the Ripper. Then she marked my stomach with some type of red substance. She told me that is where they would cut. I thought to myself, what a waste of time preparing me for something I had no intention of going through with.

Then in came yet another nurse and told me to relax she was just going to clean me. At that point, I thought finally they would clean me up from this substance I was laying in. Wrong again, she meant she was planning on cleaning me out by placing in a catheter. I nearly jumped off the table at which point she informed me that she would now have to do it all over again.

Throughout all of this I began to get hysterical. I kept on insisting that I would have the baby by myself, just let everyone leave me alone. To my surprise, my doctor finally arrived. I started to cry the minute I saw him and told him how they were torturing me both physically and mentally. He went out into the hall and had a conference with the other doctors. He came back in and said he would have to examine me. I winced at the idea, but at that point I had no choice. This was number ten internal within the last three and half hours. It was amazing that this time I didn't feel a thing because he had such a soft touch. That infuriated me because those other animals rearranged my insides.

After the examination, he said that he thought we should wait awhile. I was happy to hear that, although I still was on the verge of a nervous breakdown. I was shaking from head to toe, the tears involuntarily running down my cheeks. As soon as my doctor left, in came a man who introduced himself as the Anesthesiologist. I told him that I had no use for him because there was no way I was going to be cut. He began to laugh and said I had no choice. He told me that my doctor had been out voted and they were going to perform the operation. I said, "Doesn't my vote count for anything?" They all shouted, "NO." That echoed in my ears. There was no way I was going to cooperate with this sadist.

He showed me a piece of paper and explained that this was the release for the C-Section. All this time, he had been yelling at me. I think that he thought that it was the best way to handle a hysterical woman in labor on the verge of a nervous breakdown and a coronary. I would have very much appreciated it if he would have showed a little compassion. He shook me and said, "You have to sign it." He then took my hand, forced a pen in it and moved my hand back and forth until finally he said, "There you signed it." I then totally lost myself into hysteria. I began to scream, shake, cry and kick all at once. This wonderful person known as the Anesthesiologist took his hand and smacked me across the face. I was stunned and I am glad to say so was my doctor who had just returned from changing into the hospital greens. He demanded that everyone leave the room immediately. Finally, I was in contact with someone with compassion. After being in the hospital for hours and encountering so many uncaring people, it was nice to know that I could regain some faith in the human race again.

My doctor told me my husband was on his way back to the hospital. He wanted to know if I wanted to see him. My first thought was no, but then I quickly changed my mind and said yes. I was finally left all alone. A few minutes later, I heard my husband's voice from the hall and my plan to save me was beginning to go into action.

As he and the doctor and nurse came into my room, I lay very still pretending to sleep. The doctor and the nurse both agreed that this was the best thing for me. They told him the absolute hell I had been through. When no one was looking at me, I took a peek at what my husband looked like in his hospital greens. He has a squeamish stomach. He gets nauseous watching Marcus Welby. I guess at that point in my life I must have looked pretty awful and the whole atmosphere of the labor room was enough to make someone with a strong stomach sick. When I looked at him it was hard to tell where the green hospital gown stopped and his neck began. He was totally green.

The doctor said to him that he had to leave. He asked if he could just give me one kiss. The doctor agreed, and what a big mistake that was. My eyes were closed shut as he bent over and kissed my cheek. I got him by the neck and screamed, "If you let them cut me, I'll kill you." I was holding on to his neck for dear life because remember I had a strong flow of adrenaline and the doctor and the nurse had to help my husband release my grip. They were at a loss for words and my husband was at a loss for breath. They had to sit him down and give him some water. I could just see the headlines in front of me. "Woman in labor does not stoop so low as to curse her husband for what he has done, she just proceeds to kill him in labor room between contractions." They carefully escorted my husband out, by wheelchair, and that was the last I had see of him until it was all over.

Chapter 18

The contractions and the accompanying pain still continued, but now much more frequently. I am happy to report that from that time on my doctor stayed by my side.

He sat next to the slab I was laying on holding my hand and wiping my forehead. If I had a contraction, he unlike the others, believed me. He did not let anyone else touch me, or even come into the room. I began to feel sorry for him, after all, he had to sit there and listen to my groans and moans.

Periodically, the other interns and doctors peeked into the room and wanted to know how long he was going to wait until he preformed the C-section. He insisted that he knew what he was doing and that I would be perfectly alright. Thank God someone had faith in me. Another thing I was thankful for, he did not give me anymore internals. He felt that if he left me alone, nature would take its course. And finally it did.

All at once I had a strange feeling inside of me. I thought to myself, "How could I have to move my bowels at a time like this?" I decided not to make a further fool out of myself, so I kept quiet. I couldn't keep quiet for long, because the pressure became too great.

In a very low voice, I whispered to the doctor, "I think I have to move my bowels." He jumped up, took a quick feel of my stomach and then, finally, after waiting nine months and many torturous hours in the hospital, I heard the words I had so longingly been waiting to hear. The doctor said, "Get a stretcher in here, the baby is coming."

Chapter 19

The doctor's orders were followed immediately. A group of interns, nurses and other hospital like personnel came running. With my doctor finally in charge, they did not have the nerve to tell me to get on the stretcher myself. Instead, they gently eased me onto the waiting chariot that would carry me into the sterile room where a new life would begin.

Once in my new surroundings, I was greeted by my favorite, the anesthesiologist. He said, "Oh no, not you again." I said, "Believe me, the feeling is mutual."

I was then placed on the table, I did hope that it would be my last stop. A sheet was placed over me and my feet were placed in stirrups. At this point I felt that I would have made a terrific attraction in the side show of the Barnum and Bailey Circus.

The anesthesiologist took his place behind me and leaned over and placed a mask over my face. He said, "Breathe normally." I said, "Why should I be able to breathe normally, nothing else has been normal since I got here." He is telling me to breathe normally, the doctor is telling me when I have a contraction to bear down, and the nurse standing next to me said I must have had a hard time because I looked like hell. With all these comments, I barely knew what was happening.

Every time I felt a contraction I followed instructions exactly to bear down. As the pains got stronger, I found it harder to breathe. I thought, well at least now maybe Mr. Cool standing behind me with the oxygen mask could finally be of some help.

Wrong again, he did have the mask on me, but around my neck, not any place near my nose and mouth. I have to admit that the mask started off in the right place, but after bearing down so much I guess the mask moved. Unfortunately, I was the only one aware of this fact. The anesthesiologist was so busy trying to make it with the nurse that he did not pay any attention to me. As he heard me having trouble breathing, he started the oxygen and then proceeded to ask the doctor if he could take care of another patient. Through all this, I might have lost my self control at times, and my self respect, but thank goodness I did not lose my sense of humor. I shouted to him as he was leaving the room, "Hey, what do I look like chopped liver. The oxygen is not doing my Adams Apple any good. Please place the mask over my mouth and nose." I have to admit that this brought a lot of attention to me. The doctor started balling him out and then decided that he should talk to him later.

Now that I was finally breathing more normally, I did finally get the knack of bearing down to a science. I heard the doctor say, "Just a little bit more." There was a feeling inside of me that was wonderful. I felt the baby coming out. It was like I was being divided into two human beings. I shall never forget that feeling.

I think that the shock was too much for me, because the next thing I remember is a nurse taking my finger prints. I said, "What happened?" The nurse replied, "I heard they gave you a hard time and visa versa, but how could you forget what happened." She said, "You had a baby." I said, "Yes, that much I know, you see I was pregnant when they admitted me. What did I have?" "Oh, I'll have to check," she said. Nothing was going right yet.

Minutes later she returned and said you have a normal healthy little girl. I said, "No, not me, they kept on telling me that it was a boy all the way through labor." She said, "Mistakes are made. Believe me it is a beautiful girl." I was in shock. There were no girls born in my family since I was born, that included cousins. My husband's family was notorious for boys. How lucky could I be, A GIRL. We had picked out the name Tammy for a girl but hadn't decided on a middle name. When the nurse asked me what the baby's name was, I said without hesitation, "Tammy Joy," because for the first time in hours I finally had some JOY.

Chapter 20

By now the time was about 7:30 a.m. I was brought to a room, and gently placed in a bed. In my mind, I knew I had just had a baby, but the reality hadn't hit me yet. I was extremely confused and I called the nurse to ask if they had removed the catheter. The nurse looked and said there was nothing there. I asked her how my C-section went. She lifted the cover and said either I had some special kind of healing power and the scar completely disappeared within one hour, or I did not have a C-section. I chose to go along with the later thought. I remembered that my daughter had made the grand entrance into the world all by herself, with just a little help from me.

All of a sudden I remembered that my parents did not know that I had given birth. I reached over and picked up the phone and called my mother. She answered the phone by saying that whoever it was she could not talk because her daughter had just given birth and she was rushing around to get ready to go to the hospital. I couldn't get a word in edge wise and she practically hung up before I was able to properly identify myself as her daughter, the new mother. Between the tears we both realized how happy we were. Of course, my mother was upset that she wasn't there for the whole thing. I told her that if Howie, my husband had the choice, he wouldn't have been there. That's the difference between a husband and the mother of the expectant mother.

The next call I made was to my boss. It was about 7:45 now and considering the fact that she was never on time for work during the five years I worked for her, I knew I would be waking her, but who cared. I did wake her and since I had already given my job up I had nothing to lose. She couldn't believe that it was actually me, but of course she was so happy for me.

Chapter 21

When I hung up that phone, I realized that I hadn't eaten for many hours and that I was hungry. When the nurse came in I asked for some breakfast. The more she brought in the more I asked for. Before I was through, I had eaten two bowls of frosted flakes, four buttered rolls, two scrambled eggs and two cups of coffee. I guess I kind of forgot that I wasn't eating for two anymore.

After the breakfast and the other babies were put back in the nursery, they let my husband in. When he walked in, he looked terrible. I thought to myself, if he looks like that what must I look like after the previous six hours of torture.

It was clear to see through all the tiredness on my husband's face the joy he was experiencing. As I am writing this, I too can recall that wonderful moment, he said, "She is normal, healthy, beautiful and most important of all, she's ours."

I felt a little jealously, because he had seen her and I had not. He described her as being light skinned, big blue eyes, light brown hair, a little nose and a beautifully shaped mouth.

The nurse then came in and asked my husband to leave. To be honest I was now getting a little tired and was looking forward to a peaceful sleep.

Now, I felt my cloud that I was floating on come down to earth, because I did begin to feel quite a bit of pain. I think that the only part of my body that did not hurt was my hair.

The pain pills that were given to me had finally taken effect at about 11:00 when they woke me to ask me if I wanted lunch. I told them that I had just given birth 5 hours before (as if they didn't know) and did they think I would get nauseous if I ate. They advised me of the fact that I was the talk of the maternity ward because of the huge breakfast I had consumed and assured me that it would be perfectly alright if I ate my lunch.

I couldn't wait to finish eating because then I knew that they would bring me my daughter. That moment finally came. I was carefully propped up in bed and they handed me my baby.

The only problem I had excepting this moment was that this baby did not look anything like the one my husband had so vividly described to me. This little one had dark hair, dark complexion and dark eyes. Then, for the shock of my life, I pulled away the diaper and discovered a penis.

Uncontrollably, I screamed for the nurse who insisted that they do not make mistakes like that (this was through an intercom). I demanded that she come in. When she did, I wanted to know in what anatomy book is it written that little baby girls are first born with a penis. She looked in shock and scooped that baby up and ran out of the room. I did not know what to do first, so I prayed that this whole thing was not a dream and I truly had a daughter.

Moments later the head nurse came in carrying another bundle, apologized and handed me this beautiful form of nature wrapped in a pink blanket and all at once I knew that this was our Tammy Joy.

Chapter 22

As most new mothers feel the first time they hold their newborn child, I felt as if it could not be possible. The tiny fingers, little nose and mouth, and big blue eyes all put together made a helpless little person, who at this time was totally dependent on me. But, who was I. I had always been somebody's daughter, then somebody's wife. Now, for the first time I would be in charge of somebody.

My first responsibility to this small bundle of joy would be to give her the bottle. The nurse brought in a four ounce bottle filled with formula and Tammy playfully started to drink. It was like a dream world. My thoughts ran in all directions. How would I comb her hair (if she had any)? What would she wear to come home? How could I possibly manage by myself? Still through all these thoughts, I felt that this was just a wonderful dream.

Then, the reality hit me. A loud noise from the bottom of this neatly wrapped bundle and a stream of green watery liquid oozing down my leg. How thrilling, her first bowel movement and it had to be all over her mother. I laughed to myself, forgive her she didn't know what she was doing. As I picked her up, she had this strange look on her face as she gagged and proceeded to give me back all four ounces that I was so proud that she had finished. All over my back and hair was this warm brownish smelly liquid.

The nurse then walked in and started to laugh. "How do you like motherhood?" She was able to blurt out through the laughter. I refused to let her hear any complaints, so I said, "It is just what I expected it to be."

Then she asked me for the bottle. When I handed her the empty bottle she wanted to know what happened to the rest of the formula. I told her that the baby drank it. She turned white as a ghost. She had the nerve to scream at me because the baby was only supposed to drink 1 ounce for the first day. I demanded to know why no one had told me that and of course then her tune changed and she apologized.

I told her not to fear, because I am sure that if they rang out my hair and my nightgown they would have recovered the missing three ounces of formula.

I gave my daughter a kiss good-bye and I was now left alone to get myself back into some kind of order.

Chapter 23

I thought that I would be by myself, but wrong again. When you are in the hospital, I think that they use you for experiments. From the time they took my daughter away, they took my temperature, blood and urine. I had a few minutes to eat supper and then it was time to feed the baby again.

This time with the right directions on feeding and burping everything went like clockwork. She ate, drank and burped just like a pro. Such a bright child I thought to myself.

Moments after they took her away it was time for visiting. In walked my husband still glowing, followed by my parents and my sister. After the kissing and the hugging and the many tears of happiness, they all left me alone to visit the princess in the glass enclosed nursery. I thought to myself how unfair, I wanted to be there too. Bravely I swung my feet over the side of the bed, dangled my feet and planted them on the ground.

I could not believe that it only had been about 12 hours since the last time I had attempted to do the death defying stunt of walking. It was more like a crotch-crawl step. I felt that after what I had been through a little walk could not be so hard. Wrong again. It was torture. I eased my way into the hall hoping that someone would be there to help me. It was like I was invisible, no one stopped at all. I was a big girl now, a mother. I would do it by myself. Slowly, very slowly, using the wall as a huge crutch I inched my way to the nursery.

Finally, in the far off distance, about ten feet away, I saw the large crowd of happy faces banging on the windows trying to arouse the sleeping infants. Closer and closer I got. At this point, I could imagine how a person coming to the finish line of the 26 mile marathon felt. As I got closer, I saw my family, not that they could have cared less about seeing me. The chatter of the visitors got louder and they were all raving about a baby who was raising her head and moving from side to side. They were all saying how beautiful and alert she was.

When I reached my husband, parents and sister from the expressions on their face I realized that my Tammy Joy was the center of attention. From the look on my loved ones faces and then when I looked at my daughter, I could not remember how I had gotten to the nursery nor did I care how I would get back. At that point, I realized that happiness and joy were the best pain killers in the world.

Chapter 24

After my exhausting adventure during the visiting hour, I looked forward to a quiet restful night. I forgot one little thing, Tammy, who they brought into me to feed.

When the nurse left us alone, my roommate whispered mysteriously to me, "Look what I have." I glanced over and saw a camera. I thought to myself, what's the big deal. She then went on to explain that it was a Polaroid camera and that we could have instant pictures of the baby.

Being the law abiding citizen that I am, I hesitated because there were signs all over the place that no pictures of the baby were allowed to be taken. She explained to me that this was her fourth child and she had always taken pictures. The only reason why they did not want you to take pictures was because they wanted you to buy the hospital pictures. The hospital pictures were the ones that made all babies look the same as if they were 21 inches tall and 95 year olds.

My roommate was very convincing and before I knew it I was posing this tiny bundle of diapers and blankets against my pillows. I really felt guilty. This feeling reminded me of the time when I was ten years old and removed the label on the pillow that said do not remove and a long list of punishments under it. I remember something about the Federal Government being involved. Well, I did remove such a label and for months after that I feared for my life.

How could this be the same? The Federal Government had nothing to do with my baby. I was paying to stay in the hospital and I paid to have the baby so what could happen.

Well, finally after about ten minutes of adjusting and readjusting the baby, with my roommate as the look-out, the picture was taken. Breathlessly I waited the minute until the picture developed itself. There it finally was, a picture of fluffy white pillows and a pink blanket. Tammy was not to be seen. Well, it wasn't a total loss. I did get a picture of the bed.

We then heard the nurses coming back down the hall and we realized that through all the picture taking, we did not have a chance to feed the babies. I handed back a full bottle to the nurse and said, "I guess that she was too tired to eat." The nurse told me not to worry that when she woke up they would feed her. That was a load off my mind, now all I had to worry about was if they would find the evidence of the picture and throw me out in the cold. After thinking about it, I felt safe because the hospital bill was so much that the longer they kept you there the better.

I got myself situated as comfortably as possible in the bed and went to sleep with a smile on my face with fond memories of the past day's events.

Chapter 25

I was in such a peaceful sleep when at 6:30 a.m. I was woken up to have my temperature taken and to be given some pills. They brought me in a breakfast tray consisting of watery scrambled eggs, dried cereal with milk, coffee and a pastry. I was very hungry and finished everything like a good girl. Then my roommate said, "Remember, don't have the milk." "Too late," I replied. I wasn't sure why. She told me that milk starts to flow into your breasts and you shouldn't have milk products. Another thing the hospital forgot to tell me. Well, at least they were now bringing me the right baby.

After I had fed Tammy her breakfast, I decided to take a shower. I swung my legs over the bed, dangled my feet and started to stand up. It was not any easy task, but I was determined. I was now in an upright position and I realized that the hemorrhoids that I had during pregnancy must have multiplied during the past two days. It was as if another person was living inside of me and trying to push their way out of the opposite end of where a baby comes out (get the picture).

It was a good thing that the shower was right across from my room because if it were any further I could not have made it. The shower was quite refreshing, but I was very happy to be back in my bed again and I took a short nap.

Soon it was lunch time. This hospital must have cornered the market on chickens, because the supper before was chicken soup and chicken and for lunch it was chicken salad. The menu for the following two days was similar. The hospital dietician provided more ways to serve bland chicken than you could possibly think of. I told everyone who was coming to visit me to bring me FOOD.

My afternoon visitors consisted of a corned beef sandwich and a chocolate cream pie. I was so hungry that to this day I can't remember which of my friends came, only that they supplied me with food.

Before I went to sleep that night, my roommate told me I better ask for ice packs. From the look on my face, she went on to explain that my breasts would be very swollen in the morning and the ice packs would help.

I mentioned to the nurse that I would like icepacks and she said when she got a chance. I felt no harm in asking, but I was sure that I would not get them.

I was uncomfortable during the night and was not in a very deep sleep. When I opened my eyes, I screamed. There were these two huge hands on my breasts. The nurse came running in. I thought I was being attacked. Boy, did I feel like a fool. The nurse put the light on an assured me that I was perfectly safe. After all, she said, what harm can two rubber gloves stuffed with ice do. So, those were the ice packs, how clever.

Chapter 26

The next morning I had a slight temperature. Of course, being the nervous person that I am, I thought that this was the end of the line for me. The nurse told me not to worry that this morning I could still feed the baby, but if I still had it at lunch they would have to look into the situation. I told her about my experience of being attacked by ice packs during the night and I am sure that my nerves had cause the fever.

I was lucky that when the nurse took my temperature at lunch she left me alone. I had worked myself into such a nervous state that I had broken out into a rash. To hide this new condition of mine, I wrapped a nightgown around my neck and wore it like an ascot. I know I looked ridiculous, but at least there wasn't any inquiry about my rash. I looked at the thermometer and saw that it was slightly over 100. I quickly shook it down and down to 94. I was getting desperate. I remembered that I once saw on television that a nurse took someone's temperature by sticking the thermometer under the patients arm. So that's what I did and I felt like I hit the jackpot. The mercury read 98.6. What a break. I could not look the nurse in the face when she read the thermometer, but who cared, I was considered normal, (at least temperature wise).

My entire family came to visit everyday and all in all the hospital stay was going pretty fast. In the back of my mind, I kept on having flashes of the horrible experience in the labor room, but now that it was behind me I was more or less able to handle it.

By the time the fourth day arrived, my stitches were beginning to really bother me. The doctor said that it was normal because I was healing. I had to sit on a rubber tube and I thought that this would be part of me for the rest of my life.

Each time I moved I felt that I was being pulled closer and closer to the ground. I thought that if only I could wear knee pads and crawl around on my hands and knees, I would be O.K.

The day finally arrived when I was to begin my new life as a mother at home. My doctor came in that morning and cut my stitches. What a relief that was, I could now stand up straight and tall.

All through my stay in the hospital at every opportunity I had I complained to my doctor. I remember the last thing I said to him that day in the hospital that thanks to all I went through Tammy Joy would be an only child.

He said to me, "I've heard that before, I'll bet you'll be back in this maternity ward soon."

My husband and mother then came into the room. The nurse brought the baby in dressed in a beautiful hand knitted sweater and hat lovingly made by my mother. Off I was to become in my eyes Mother of the Year. In the back of my mind, I kept on hearing my doctor's words. You'll be back.

EPILOGUE

Diane Leyden did return as her doctor predicted. A little more than three years later she gave birth to her second daughter, Hope Robyn.

It is with JOY and HOPE that we live our lives. We are grateful to our mother for leaving us this precious gift.

CPSIA information can be obtained
at www.ICGtesting.com
Printed in the USA
BVOW11s1507310717

490707BV00007B/54/P

9 781942 500346